"If poetry doesn't make anything happen, at least poetry this well written and focused, this concise and yet comprehensive, provides an ethical, moral, and aesthetic compass. Truth and true poetry, hard to come by, but in David Starkey's book it keeps us from forgetting the lies and corporate self-serving cant—damage to the language and our country—we have endured. This kind of poetry keeps our collective shoulder to the wheel."

CHRISTOPHER BUCKLEY, AUTHOR OF *STAR JOURNAL: SELECTED POEMS*

"Many of us asked, 'Wait, what just happened?!' with increasing alarm, outrage, and exhaustion over the course of Donald J. Trump's term in office. Now David Starkey offers an unexpected and strangely satisfying answer in *What Just Happened: 210 Haiku Against the Trump Presidency*. At the rate of seventeen syllables per week (a sly echo of the character constraint of a Tweet), Starkey's tonally dexterous poems both chronicle and satirize the Trump years. The result is a book that renders the burden of not forgetting not only more bearable but less bleak—a modest miracle."

CATHERINE ABBEY HODGES, AUTHOR OF *INSTEAD OF SADNESS*

"Here's a book of high-speed history for you, friends. It's easy to forget the Trump years, probably because we want to. But if we are to remember the past so as not to repeat it, David Starkey makes it easy and even pleasant to do so by wrapping each of the president's gaffes in that most durable of poetical forms, the haiku. 'Literature is news that stays news,' says Pound, and Starkey proves his point with poems that are funny, maddening, and razor-sharp."

DAVID KIRBY, AUTHOR OF *GET UP, PLEASE: POEMS*

About the Author

David Starkey is Founding Director of the Creative Writing Program at Santa Barbara City College and Co-editor of Gunpowder Press and *The California Review of Books*. A former Poet Laureate of Santa Barbara, he has published poetry in *American Scholar, Georgia Review, Prairie Schooner, Southern Review* and many others. His textbook, *Creative Writing: Four Genres in Brief* (Bedford/St. Martin's) is in its fourth edition, and his recent poetry collections include *A Few Things You Should Know About the Weasel, Circus Maximus, Like a Soprano* and *Dance, You Monster, to My Soft Song*.

You can read more about him at *davidstarkey.net*.

What
Just
Happened

210 Haiku
Against the Trump Presidency
a satire

David Starkey

www.vineleavespress.com

For Sandy

*"If a restaurant is dirty on the outside,
it is dirty on the inside!"*
Donald J. Trump, 25 June 2018

2017

winter

Alternative facts
make their first of many star
turn appearances.

No, says Enrique
Peña Nieto, Mexico
won't pay for the wall.

Neil Gorsuch will fill
a seat that has been empty
for almost a year.

Close call on school
choice zealot Betsy DeVos.
Mike Pence breaks the tie.

David Starkey

The president tells
Comey, re Flynn, "I hope
you can let this go."

Jeff Sessions backs new
private prisons: invest now
in concrete and steel.

The ethics course
for all new White House staff is
eliminated.

spring

Kellyanne trumpets
Ivanka's failing fashion
line on *Fox & Friends*.

Rachel Maddow airs
leaked tax returns. Pretty sure
he's no billionaire.

Is Devin Nunes
a better dairy farmer
than a spy? Barely.

Wielding a Bible,
Sessions calls sanctuary
cities immoral.

The president looks
uneasy walking with Xi
at Mar-a-Lago.

"We're like your taxes:
unpaid," an activist claps
back on Tax March day.

He forgets to place
his hand on his heart; a nudge
from his annoyed wife.

"Media outlets
like MSNBC are
fake news. They're fake news."

"ObamaCare is
a lie and it is dead!" he
opines on Twitter.

For "refusing to
admit his errors," Comey
is canned on TV.

He snags the Collar
of Abdulaziz Al Saud
and signs an arms deal.

"We must take our fate,"
grumbles Angela Merkel,
"into our own hands."

A "self-inflicted
major economic wound":
Au revoir, Paris.

summer

Five months gone, his wife
and son finally move in.
No one's overjoyed.

Super-cautious Robert
Mueller investigates. Does
he dare eat a peach?

"Carbon dioxide
does not cause climate change," says
expert Rick Perry.

Mounting the rostrum,
Sarah Huckabee Sanders,
furious in pearls.

What was said in that
very private tête-à-tête
with smirking Putin?

Don, Jr.: "A high-
quality person" known for
"his transparency."

Scaramucci on
Steve Bannon: "I'm not trying
to suck my own cock."

At the Jamboree:
"A scout is loyal—we could
use some more of that."

"Look at Hillary
Clinton's 33,000
deleted emails."

Of Charlottesville, he
remarks: "there were very fine
people on both sides."

After Charlottesville,
even the CEOs need
to take a breather.

Sheriff Joe accepts
his pardon like any red-
blooded patriot.

Post-Harvey comments:
"They were just happy. It's nice.
It's been beautiful."

fall

In the gutter, hand-
written on a wet cardboard
sign: *Defend DACA*.

Excellent news: Mar-
a-Lago is unhurt by
Hurricane Irma.

At the UN: bright
blue tie and a promise to
destroy Rocket Man.

NFL players
taking a knee? He'd fire the
proud sons of bitches.

In Puerto Rico,
hurricane survivors get
a gift: paper towels!

The president dares
Tillerson: "Compare IQs.
I'm not a moron."

The pregnant Gold Star
widow is scolded: "He knew
what he signed up for."

Melania: "Eat
lunch with someone you don't know.
Be kind. Don't bully."

Manafort and Gates
are charged with conspiracy,
but "NO COLLUSION!"

In indigo silk
shirts, he and Putin look dressed
for Christopher Street.

A grin. Skin pockmarked.
Duterte extends a moist
hand, and he shakes it.

Born magnanimous,
with a wave he pardons this
year's turkey, Drumstick.

At an observance
honoring Navahos, a
Pocahontas joke.

winter

At what cost, the new
capital of Israel?
O Jerusalem!

Roy Moore's too loathsome
even for Alabama.
"I knew he would lose."

The gingerbread White
House in the East Dining Room
is melting, melting.

Poor Barron: awkward,
tall and shy, endlessly in
his father's shadow.

2018

"He not only lost
his job"—the sly, gin-blossomed
one—"he lost his mind."

He much prefers blondes
from Norway to immigrants
from "shithole countries."

"Incredibly good
genes and that's just the way God
made him"—his doctor.

"No," he admits on
ITV, "I wouldn't say
I'm a feminist."

Despite Chinese tricks,
ice caps didn't melt: "They're at
a record level."

"Like death," "treasonous":
the un-Americans who did
not applaud his speech.

Nine months with playmate
Karen McDougal squelched with
a modest kill fee.

His response to the
massacre at Mandalay
Bay: no more bump stocks.

Fact: Melania
came to America on
an Einstein visa.

spring

His ex-aide Nunberg's
not alone in calling his
boss "an idiot."

Stormy will pay back
the 130K
if they'll let her talk.

Stormy passes a
lie detector test. How will
the president do?

David Starkey

America gets
some bad news: every day is
now April Fool's Day.

When you're the head of
the EPA, you need a sound-
proof telephone booth.

"It's an attack on
our country in a true sense"—
the raid on Cohen.

Does he ever sleep,
or are his dark nights consumed
composing vile tweets?

Another visit
from Angela Merkel: this
time he shakes her hand.

In the Rose Garden
he makes a dubious case for
the power of prayer.

Without apparent
irony, Melania
commences *Be Best*.

Just look what kindness
has begot: "These aren't people.
These are animals."

On the links with Yes-
Man Lindsey Graham: he knows he'll
never lose a round.

Cadet Bonespurs lays
a wreath. The Unknown Soldier—
ha, what a loser!

summer

The Eagles don't want
to come to the White House? Fine,
they're disinvited.

The North Korean
nuclear threat has ended,
vows the president.

I really don't care
do u? Melania's green
parka speaks volumes.

Without ICE, you are
"going to be afraid to
walk out of your house."

How many scandals
does it take to drive Pruitt
out? Answer: Fifteen.

At Windsor Castle,
he leaves the doddering old
Queen eating his dust.

"US foolishness
and stupidity" tweet liked
by @VPutin.

Recording of call
between Cohen and himself:
"Cash?" "Check?" "Have to pay."

He TiVos his own
rallies, rewatches them when
poll numbers are down.

He displays a toy
astronaut while explaining
why we need Space Force.

Of Omarosa:
"crazed, crying lowlife." Also,
his dagger: "a dog."

Manafort, guilty
of tax evasion and bank
fraud, seems pretty chill.

As past presidents
mourn the loss of Senator
John McCain, he golfs.

fall

Anonymous *Times*
op-ed offers cold comfort:
"adults in the room."

On board Air Force One,
9/11. He dreams of
crowds, pretends to pray.

Fifteen hundred kids
are missing at the border.
He hasn't seen them.

His boy Kavanaugh
doesn't remember much, but
he sure loves his beer.

M. takes great selfies
in her white pith helmet while
touring Africa.

Saudi involvement
in Khashoggi's death? Well, um:
"Nobody knows yet."

The poor House of Saud:
railroaded like Kavanaugh;
they deny it too.

"Screw your optics"—
Bowers enters the Tree of
Life—"I'm going in."

Daily FOX shocks: this
caravan of human beings
surely means us harm.

"A Big Victory,"
despite Democrats flipping
41 House seats.

They need to "get smart,"
West Coast cities like Pleasure—
make that Paradise.

Ivanka's vs.
Hillary's emails? "A whole
different…all fake news."

Glory days are gone,
the Boss declares: "He's deeply
damaged at his core."

winter

Stonewalling Roger
Stone has "guts," but throw the book
at fickle Cohen.

Zinke resigns to
the immense relief of all
creatures great and small.

James "Mad Dog" Mattis
calls it quits: the general
is not *that* crazy.

A hall of scary
red Christmas trees and *Be Best*
pencil ornaments.

David Starkey

2019

John Kelly resigns:
this gig is way harder than
being a Marine.

The camera loves
new star AOC. *Damn.* Can
you say, "Jealousy"?

The Clemson Tigers
are fêted with Burger King,
Wendy's, Dominos.

He sets a record:
fastest visit to Doctor
King's Memorial.

With bitter cold in
the Midwest, he fake-pleads for
"Global Waming" [sic].

He livestreams the names
of donors during State of
the Union Address.

Enter William Barr,
renowned for independence
and integrity.

Not Russia, the "true
ENEMY OF THE PEOPLE"
is *The New York Times*.

A two-hour speech at
CPAC. There's nothing like a
friendly audience.

spring

The fast food schtick worked
with Clemson. Why not reprise
with North Dakota State?

He's never wrong: "Cook,"
he claims he whispered when he
spoke of "Tim Apple."

That bastard McCain,
even dead, keeps plaguing him:
"I wasn't a fan."

Fake news had it all
wrong when they claim he canceled
Special Olympics.

"Best thing that ever
happened to Puerto Rico
is Donald J. Trump."

She was so at ease
talking deportation, ex-
Homeland boss Nielsen.

In Barr's opinion,
There's nothing to see here, folks.
Move it right along.

The way he spins it,
if he's not locked in jail, he
must be innocent.

Barr is a big guy.
He hunkers through his Senate
hearing: *Nope. Nope. Nope.*

Sometimes he just sits
and stews while the stylist works
keenly on his hair.

He's quite taken with
Orbán, who's made more headway
on *his* ethnostate.

Three minutes is all
he can stomach with Schumer
and Crazy Nancy.

Mueller, by his own
admission, could have done more
but didn't. Thanks, Bob.

summer

The mayor of London's
like NYC's: "very dumb…
only half his height."

Will she be missed, Ms.
Sarah Huckabee Sanders?
No, she won't be missed.

126

If reelected,
he will "cure cancer and end
AIDS." Any questions?

127

Twenty steps into
North Korea with his bud:
two clods in a pod.

128

Independence Day:
military flyovers,
moneyed VIPs.

129

To the Squad: "IF YOU
ARE NOT HAPPY HERE YOU CAN
LEAVE!"—But they're *from* here.

Of his previous
Squad tweetstorm: *not a racist*
bone in his body.

A perfect call to
Ukraine: "I would like you to
do us a favor."

In Cincinnati,
he riles up the crowd: middle-
aged piddlers, booing.

The shootings in El
Paso and Dayton were bad,
but gun control? *Nah.*

Time for the States to
step up its real estate game.
Is Greenland for sale?

"Lack of knowledge or
great disloyalty": Jews who
vote for Democrats.

At a meeting on
climate change, his bleak emblem
is an empty chair.

fall

Hurricane Tracker-
in-Chief flaunts super-human
skills with his Sharpie.

A big old place
like Alaska? Surely there's
lots of room to drill.

Zuckerberg visits
the Oval Office to chat.
Washington looks on.

With the gavel's sharp
rap, the formal impeachment
inquiry begins.

His tremendous new
plan for the Southern border:
alligator moats.

"Nancy Pelosi
hates America." Why else
would she impeach him?

His Florida golf
resort was perfect for a
G-7 summit.

Kurds abandoned to
die in Syria. Even
Lindsey is ashamed.

Fans chanting, "Lock *him*
up!" at the World Series. He
never liked baseball.

"Such a farce. Big hoax.
Totally unfounded Witch
Hunt. Dishonest scam."

What kind of a creep
would set out to smear Marie
Yovanovitch? *Hmmm.*

There are so many
witnesses against him. Could
they *all* be lying?

A federal judge
rules: "Presidents are not kings."
He begs to differ.

winter

His corpulent pal
in Pyongyang now styles him an
"impatient old man."

The articles of
impeachment are ratified.
He holds a rally.

Christianity
Today blasts his "profoundly
immoral actions."

He tweets the whistle-
blower's name, like a butcher
throwing dogs raw meat.

2020

Orange makeup can't
hide the fact that he now looks
a million years old.

Bolton will talk if
the Senate subpoenas him.
An empty offer.

Ken Starr joins his team.
The same Starr who said Clinton
was a hypocrite.

The first virus case
in the United States. He
says: "We do have a plan."

The Senate votes *No
Witnesses.* They've already
made their decision.

Rush Limbaugh receives
the Presidential Medal
of Freedom. Honest!

He predicts it will
become "weaker with warmer
weather, then gone." *Gone.*

The situation
with the virus is "very
much under control."

"Within a couple
days it is going to be
down close to zero."

spring

"Anybody that
wants a test can get a test.
The tests are perfect."

"We're doing a great
job with it. Just stay calm and
it will go away."

"They think August, it
could be July." A pause. "Could
be longer than that."

"By Easter Sunday
you will have packed churches all
over our country."

"So, with the masks, it's
a voluntary thing. You
don't have to do it."

Looking at him, you
can tell he's an expert at
almost everything.

Sweet, sweet pandemic
that makes everyone watch him
daily on TV.

Ultraviolet
light might knock this virus out.
And disinfectant.

One million cases.
Fifty thousand dead. Time to
open things back up.

"We can put out—I
call them 'embers,' or a fire—
we could put it out."

In the ICUs,
his devoted voters are
drowning on dry land.

He's heard a lot of
good stories about this hy-
droxychloroquine.

He's hunkered down in
a bunker as protestors
chant the name *George Floyd*.

summer

Is that *his* Bible
he's holding at St. John's Church?
Well, it's *a* Bible.

That old man was an
ANITFA provocateur
thrown down by the cops.

His Tulsa rally
poorly attended, he blames
no-shows on "Kung Flu."

He walks the border
wall near Yuma: this thing of
steel is "beautiful."

Russia financed hits
by Taliban on US
soldiers. No biggie.

Three million cases.
Good time to withdraw from the
WHO.

A panel for folks
positively impacted
by law enforcement.

The nightly Portland
protests are worse, he reckons,
than Afghanistan.

Is there a reason
the mail has suddenly stopped
arriving on time?

"No religion, no
anything, hurt the Bible,
hurt God." Thus, Biden.

The polls, he assures
his fanatic supporters,
were wrong last time too.

Such a great treatment—
convalescent plasma, at
least that's what he hears.

Long lashes, long nails—
batshit Kimberly Guilfoyle
at the RNC.

Cops who shoot unarmed
suspects are like golfers who
choke on a short putt.

fall

He's honored to get
a Nobel Prize nod from a
Norwegian fascist.

"This China virus
was a big setback, but now
we're back to business."

Come one, come all, to
the superspreader event
in the Rose Garden.

Along with most of
his staff, he tests positive
for Covid-19.

Virtual debates
are not his forte. It's too
hard to non-stop yell.

Everywhere he goes,
his crowds urge him to greater
and greater outrage.

He leaves the *60
Minutes* set, pissed. Lesley Stahl's
questions were too hard.

The gods love dark jests:
Amy Coney Barrett in
place of RPG.

Biden wins. The Q plan
fails. His swollen pumpkin head
explodes, practically.

He never said he
would concede. In this regard,
he's good as his word.

And so the Big Steal
begins, which he claims he wants
to stop. Endless gall.

"This is a total fraud. The
Department of Justice—well,
maybe they're involved."

Rudy's star witness:
a drunk ex-stripper working
freelance in IT.

winter

The Supreme Court is
seemingly also involved
in the cover-up.

Repeat a Big Lie
enough and it becomes true,
said Joseph Goebbels.

In sympathy with
his fellow criminals, a
flurry of pardons.

The Secretary
of State in Georgia is told,
"Find the votes we need."

2021

At the Capitol,
one last traitorous assault
on democracy.

Making history
again: the first president
to be impeached twice.

Gone: like a piece of
toilet paper wiped from the
sole of someone's shoe.

Acknowledgements

While I wrote these poems in a flush of inspiration, with little feedback from other readers, *What Just Happened* would never have been possible if it weren't for decades' worth of advice and inspiration from countless friends, poets, and editors. My thanks go out to Ken Autrey, Wendy Bishop, Gudrun Bortman, Laure-Anne Bosselaar, Mary Brown, Andrei Codrescu, Kate Daniels, Michael Dennison, Jessica Faust, Cecile Goding, Richard Guzman, Rodger Kamenetz, Gerald Locklin, Perie Longo, Glenna Luschei, Marsha de la O, David Oliveira, Carolie Parker, Robert Parham, Jim Peterson, David Racine, John Ridland, Bruce Smith, James Smith, Barry Spacks, Phil Taggart, David Thomson, Paul J. Willis, George Yatchisin, Chryss Yost, and others too numerous to mention. I'm especially grateful to my late friend David Case, who first encouraged me to pursue poetry as my life's work.

Thank you also to the good folks at Vine Leaves Press, especially Jessica Bell and Amie McCracken, for believing in *What Just Happened* and transforming it from a manuscript into a beautiful book faster than you can say Twitter.

Vine Leaves Press

Enjoyed this book?
Go to *vineleavespress.com* to find more.